D0590197

SOME CLASSIC RULES OF GOLF

FOR
TRESPASS

FOREWORD BY
PETER DOBEREINER

STUDIO EDITIONS
LONDON

First published in Great Britain by
The Ariel Press, London
entitled *Some of the Rules of Golf.*

© The Ariel Press, 1966

This edition published 1993 by Studio Editions Ltd,
Princess House, 50 Eastcastle Street, London W1N 7AP

© this edition Studio Editions Ltd, 1993

Reprinted 1994

All rights reserved. This publication may not be reproduced, stored in a retrieval system, or trasmitted, in any form or by any means electronic, mechanical, photocopying, recording or otherwise, without the prior permission of the copyright holder.

Printed and bound in China

ISBN 1 85170 998 3

FOREWORD

There can hardly be a golfer alive who is not familiar with the work of Charles Crombie. Framed prints of his Perrier rules series are to be found in most clubhouses and they remain popular nearly 90 years after their first appearance, long after his companion series on motoring and cricket and his illustrations for *Punch* and *Golf Illustrated* have been forgotten.

My affection for Crombie's 24 golfing lithographs arises from the fact that he was clearly influenced by the work of my grandfather, John Hassall. Crombie (1885–1967) was Hassall's junior by 20 years and he may even have been one of his pupils, along with Harry Rowntree, Bruce Bairnsfather and Cecil Aldin. When Perrier commissioned the golf series in 1905 Crombie decided to do them as a pastiche of Hassall's highly individual style. He set his figures in the Elizabethan era, a Hassall trademark, and drew them in the distinctive style which Hassall had evolved for his posters, involving large blocks of plain colour heavily outlined in black. Whenever I look at a Crombie I can see elements of my grandfather's work and I like to think it represents an act of homage.

The Crombie series had immediate success and shortly after its appearance Royal Doulton brought out a range of pottery decorated with transfer-printed figures in the Crombie-Hassall style. When it came to framing the Rules of Golf Crombie took some liberties with the wording and numbering but in each case the spirit of the Rules is faithfully presented.

Peter Dobereiner

1992

GOLF AND DOCTOR PERRIER

I took up golf when I was 16, and for a very peculiar reason. I had just been made a prefect at school, and I was very worried about being so bad at rugger and cricket. So I went to the Headmaster and said: "Sir, now that I am a prefect, may I please be excused all games?"

"What on earth for?"

"Because, sir, it will detract from my authority if I am seen making a fool of myself on the playing fields."

The Head, a Welshman of great wisdom, took this point. "But you must take exercise, you know. Isn't there any game you like?"

"Yes, sir. I like golf." (I had never actually played at it, but had caddied several times for my mother.)

"Very well. If you promise me to play two rounds a week, I will let you off school games."

So I learnt to play golf. I never became much better at golf than at cricket or rugger, and because I usually played alone, I cheated a great deal. I missed out difficult holes. I picked out of streams when no one was looking. And, when I got to be 18, there was the great consolation of the 19th hole.

I said there was a stream running across the golf course. Occasionally I cupped my hands and drank from it. It was the first time I had ever drunk water. I mean *pure* water out of the good earth, not chlorinated (and sometimes fluoridised) tap water. Mr. C. Stone, chief water taster of the Metropolitan Water Board, who tastes 80 samples a day, would probably have described it as "fishy-weedy", but to me it had the metallic virginal taste I now associate with dry hock.

Years later, I was to taste another water from the earth, Source Perrier, at a place called Les Bouillens (which means "the bubblings") near Vergeze, 15 miles from Nimes, Provence. Here, for good geological reasons, a spring meets a source of carbonic acid gas and gets put into bottles. These bottles contain the "champagne of table waters," Perrier — a refreshing drink on its own, and an ideal mix with wine or spirits. Dr. Perrier, who discovered it, was a very French doctor. You may have noticed certain differences between doctors of various nationalities. Germans love sending you to psychiatrists. Britons chop your leg off. Americans have a new wonder-drug. But French doctors, bless their hearts, prescribe everything they can think of, and always add a bottle of water — Perrier, Evian, or Vichy. This is because the French believe that food, drink, and medicine should all be part of the same process — the painless enjoyment of life. They don't believe much in artificial drugs, patent medicines, and pills. They don't *worry* about their health (except possibly *maladie du foie*), and they aren't always looking for "instant" cures. Most of the medicines we really need are provided by nature in the form of either herbs or mineral water. I know France is full of rude-postcard jokes about "ne buvez jamais d'eau", but they mean "don't drink *tap* water!"

Dr. Perrier "collected" thermal springs much as other people collect butterflies. His spring at Vergeze, rising in the middle of vineyards, had been known to the Romans, but only in 1863 did he get it approved by the French Government, which meant a decree signed by Napoleon III. Unfortunately, he hadn't enough money to develop it. In those days, nobody thought of just bottling the water and selling it. If you found a medicinal spring, you had to build a whole spa on top of it, according to a fashion set by the Empress Eugenie, so that it could compete with Biarritz, Aix-les-Bains, Baden-Baden. Before Perrier knew what was happening, a Monsieur Granier was building bathing cabins, a hotel, a Pump Room. The project — fortunately — failed. For Perrier water is not for swimming in — it is for drinking!

There was still not enough money for development, however — until Mr. A. W. St. John Harmsworth, brother of Lord Northcliffe, the Napoleon of Fleet Street, came down from Oxford and was touring France with his tutor. They met Dr. Perrier in Nimes and were taken by him for what must have seemed an interminable walk along dusty Provencal roads to the spring.

Hot and parched when they arrived, they drank deeply. The almost icy sparkling water was a revelation, and on an impulse young Harmsworth who could not undersrand why ice-cool water should bubble like a hot geyser, said: "Doctor, I'll buy your spring and see if I can succeed where you couldn't — but it shall always bear your name."

The water was analysed in London, compared with the mineral contents of other well-known Continental spas, and found to have justified Dr. Perrier's faith.

The distinctive Perrier bottle also derives from Mr. Harmsworth, or rather from his keep-fit exercises. A considerable athlete before being paralysed in a car accident, he decided that Perrier Water should be sold in a bottle shaped like an Indian Club. He lived at Vergeze from 1906 until his death in 1933.

It is a pity that the Perrier Bottle is not shaped like a golf club, but there are certain practical difficulties in the way. However, the Indian Club bottle is so well-known at various 19th holes that it would be silly to change it.

Have a glass of water, old boy.

And so to the Golfing Cartoons which form the subject of this book. Not much is known of Charles Crombie, the artist. He contributed several times to *Punch* and other magazines of the period, but as to whether he approached St. John Harmsworth with the idea, or vice-versa, no one knows. Whichever way it happened, the cartoons proved a wonderful project and a very great success.

Crombie's drawings are delightfully naïve; his humour is innocent and in the main cheerfully childlike. Which, of course, does not really epitomise golf. For, make no mistake, Golf is no lighthearted, whimsical affair. It is not even a game, although that is what we pretend. It is hell with an occasional sprinkling of heaven. Somewhere, over the rainbow, blue birds may fly, but will that putt go down each time? No!

What's your handicap?" a player asked his opponent as they teed up on the first.

"Golf." replied the other tersely. And how many golfers did he speak for?

And what about the sportsmanship and goodfellowship it breeds? Listen to this conversation!

"I'll never play with that twerp X again, the crook!"

"Really? What's he been up to?"

"Hooked into the rough at the 3rd, just before the top of the rise. You couldn't see the green."

"I know. About a hundred and forty yards."

"Looked for his ball for about ten minutes. Both of us did. Then he said "You play yours on, or we'll have to let the next pair through. I'll look for another minute, then catch you up". So, I played a five on to the green and was just lining up the putt when, bingo, his ball plonks three feet from the pin; I miss my putt and he's won the hole. Tells me, the liar, that he'd found it just after I'd gone over the rise, and he'd played a super six iron shot. "Wish you'd been there to see it," he'd the cheek to say."

"But look here, old man, you can't be *sure*. He *might* have found it."

"Sure? course I'm sure! I had his ball in my pocket all the time."

No, golf is not a game of cricket, chaps. Nor are the jokes which circulate the golf club cheerful ones. Except for the golfer, of course! But they serve to illustrate the thraldom of the golfer to his obsession. Consider the finale of a certain medal round match. The last two players were approaching the clubhouse in an unusual manner, for one was carrying the other. The bearer dumped his burden on the steps, stood up and wiped his brow:

"Hallo, who's that?"

"Barrington Phillips!"

"What's the matter?"

"Dead!"

"No! Poor chap. When did it happen?"

"On the 14th green. Sank a 30-footer. Too much for him."

"And you carried him all the way back? Lord, that must have been terrible for you."

"You're right! Worst part was picking him up after every stroke."

Yes, death strikes frequently in golfing jokes. The hearse was moving slowly down the road; inside a bag of golf clubs rested on top of the coffin.

"Hallo, who's dead?"

"Jane Englebury."

"Jane Englebury? Didn't know she played golf."

"She didn't. That's the widower's set of clubs. He's due off the first tee at 2.30."

Another hearse, passing by the golf course this time, just where the 18th green sat hard by the road.

The golfer was lining up a twelve footer, but as the coffin passed he stood erect and silent. Now it had passed by and he bent down and sank his putt.

"God, Arthur, that was decent of you. Interrupting your concentration like that for a funeral."

"Not at all, old man; least I could do. It would have been our twentieth anniversary tomorrow."

Reasonable when you come to think of it. For, since there is nothing more certain than death, there is equally nothing more uncertain than golf. So, while death must just be accepted like divots on the fairway, or flooded greens, golf qua golf must be cherished, must be worshipped, must always be preserved.

And should at any time some cataclysm threaten its throne; with a stiff lip its acolyte, the golfer, must be prepared to sacrifice, not just his family, but even his heritage, to safeguard the sanctity of golf.

I was playing Golf one day
When the Germans landed,
All our men had run away,
All our ships were stranded,
And the thought of England's shame
Nearly put me off my game.

ALAN JENKINS
June 1966

INTRODUCTION FROM THE 1966 EDITION.

"It's aye the same in Life and Gowff
I'm stymied late and ear,
This world is but a weary howff
I'd fain be interwhere."

ANDREW LANG

COPYRIGHT OF Perrier, FRENCH NATURAL SPARKLING TABLE WATER.

"Why is it that I play at all?
Let memory remind me,
How once I smote upon my ball
And bunkuered it behind me."

ANDREW LANG

COPYRIGHT OF Perrier, FRENCH NATURAL SPARKLING TABLE WATER.

"A famous sportsman and a judge of wine"

GOLFIANA

COPYRIGHT OF Perrier, FRENCH NATURAL SPARKLING TABLE WATER.

"Golf, that gadfly game,
That maddens even the most tame."

EARL OF WEMYSS

COPYRIGHT OF Perrier, FRENCH NATURAL SPARKLING TABLE WATER.

"Art thou a rude despiser of good manners
That in civility thou seem'st so empty?"

AS YOU LIKE IT

COPYRIGHT OF Perrier, FRENCH NATURAL SPARKLING TABLE WATER.

“ ’Tis more by art than force of numerous storkes.”

POPE

COPYRIGHT OF Perrier, FRENCH NATURAL SPARKLING TABLE WATER.

“Art sure, Timothy, tis ours?
Methinks tis but a re-made.”

THE COMPLEAT GOLFER

COPYRIGHT OF Perrier, FRENCH NATURAL SPARKLING TABLE WATER.

"A conflict of interests."

COPYRIGHT OF Perrier, FRENCH NATURAL SPARKLING TABLE WATER.

"One pain is lessened by another's anguish."

ROMEO AND JULIET

COPYRIGHT OF Perrier, FRENCH NATURAL SPARKLING TABLE WATER.

"The attempt, and not the deed, confounds us."

MACBETH

COPYRIGHT OF Perrier, FRENCH NATURAL SPARKLING TABLE WATER.

"There be some sports, are painful."

THE TEMPEST

COPYRIGHT OF Perrier, FRENCH NATURAL SPARKLING TABLE WATER.

"Was there ever man had such luck."

CYMBELINE

COPYRIGHT OF Perrier, FRENCH NATURAL SPARKLING TABLE WATER.

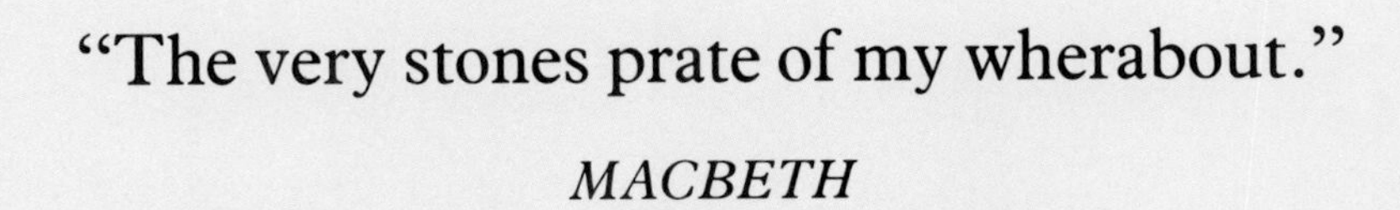
"The very stones prate of my wherabout."

MACBETH

COPYRIGHT OF Perrier, FRENCH NATURAL SPARKLING TABLE WATER.

"Never shall I forget the unearthly yell that rent the peaceful stillness of the morning."

LETTERS OF AN ANGLER

COPYRIGHT OF Perrier, FRENCH NATURAL SPARKLING TABLE WATER.

"Now up, now down, as a Bucket in a well."

CHAUCER

COPYRIGHT OF Perrier, FRENCH NATURAL SPARKLING TABLE WATER.

"Hi! Marry! Odds bodikins and gadzooks!!
have a care good varlet, have a care!"

MEMOIRS OF SIR HARRY OLIVER

COPYRIGHT OF Perrier, FRENCH NATURAL SPARKLING TABLE WATER.

"The thing they ca' The stymie a't."

ANDREW LANG

COPYRIGHT OF Perrier, FRENCH NATURAL SPARKLING TABLE WATER.

“A short straight drive.”

COPYRIGHT OF Perrier, FRENCH NATURAL SPARKLING TABLE WATER.

"The very Moudiewarts were stunned,
Nor kenned what it could mean."

ALISTER MAC ALISTER

COPYRIGHT OF Perrier, FRENCH NATURAL SPARKLING TABLE WATER.

"The harp he loved ne'er spoke again."

THE MINSTREL BOY

RULE XX
....A player ſhall not play until the ... ball iſ at reſt under penalty of one ſtroke.
COPYRIGHT OF Perrier, FRENCH NATURAL SPARKLING TABLE WATER.

"One who can
Swipe out for distance against any man,
But in what course the ball so struck may go,
No looker on — not he himself — can know."

GOLFIANA

COPYRIGHT OF Perrier, FRENCH NATURAL SPARKLING TABLE WATER.

"I am amazed! methinks, and lose my way."

KING JOHN

COPYRIGHT OF Perrier, FRENCH NATURAL SPARKLING TABLE WATER.

"Such uninterrupted exercise must beyond doubt steel the constitution against all ordinary attacks of illness."

SMOLLET ON GOLF

COPYRIGHT OF Perrier, FRENCH NATURAL SPARKLING TABLE WATER.

A man may cry 'Church, Church' at every word,
Whith no more piety than other people;
A daw's not reckoned a religious bird
Because it keeps a-cawing from a steeple."

GOLFIANA

COPYRIGHT OF Perrier, FRENCH NATURAL SPARKLING TABLE WATER.